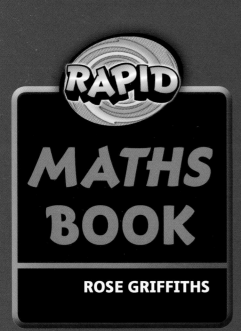

RAPID
MATHS BOOK

ROSE GRIFFITHS

Heinemann

Heinemann is an imprint of Pearson Education Limited, a company incorporated in England and Wales, having its registered office at Edinburgh Gate, Harlow, Essex, CM20 2JE. Registered company number: 872828

www.heinemann.co.uk

Heinemann is a registered trademark of Pearson Education Limited

Text © Rose Griffiths 1996, 2005, 2009

First published 1996
Second edition first published 2005
Third edition first published 2009

13 12
10 9 8 7 6 5 4

British Library Cataloguing in Publication Data
A catalogue record for this book is available from the British Library.

ISBN 978 0 435912 31 4

Designed by Anna Stasinska
Original illustrations © Pearson Education Ltd 2009
Illustrated by Martin Chatterton, Pet Gotohda and Matt Buckley
Cover illustration © Pearson Education Ltd
Cover illustration by Martin Chatterton
Printed in Malaysia (CTP-VP)

Acknowledgements
We would like to thank Kirtlington CE, Kirtlington, and Queens Dyke Primary, Witney for their invaluable help in the development and trialling of this course.

The author and publisher would like to thank the following individuals and organisations for permission to reproduce photographs:
©Shutterstock / Tania Zbrodko: p.8 and 9 (lollipop); ©Shutterstock / Elnur: p.8 and 9 (torch); ©Shutterstock / Carsten Reisinger: p.8 and 9 (safety pin); ©Pearson Education / Ben Nicholson: p.8 and 9 (1p); ©Shutterstock / Andreas68: p.8 and 9 (key); ©Shutterstock / Marcus Miranda: p.8 and 9 (2 magnet); ©Shutterstock / Joanne Harris & Daniel Bubrick: p.8 and 9 (y magnet); ©Shutterstock / Losevsky Powell: p.8 and 9 (button); ©Shutterstock / Ana de Sousa: p.8 and 9 (button 2); ©Shutterstock / Ana de Sousa: p.8 and 9 (button 3); ©Getty Images / PhotoDisk: p.8 and 9 (bus); ©Shutterstock / PeppPic: p.8 and 9 (pencil sharpener); ©Shutterstock / Jonathan Brizendine: p.8 and 9 (toy frog); ©Shutterstock / Home Studio: p.8 and 9 (string); ©Shutterstock / Pakhnyushcha: p.8 and 9 (paperclip); ©Shutterstock / Richard Sargeant: p.8 and 9 (candle); ©Pearson Education / Ben Nicholson: p.8 and 9 (2p); ©Shutterstock / Tatiana Popova: p.8 and 9 (mouse); ©Shutterstock / Albert H. Teich: p.8 and 9 (tiger); ©Getty Images / PhotoDisk: p.8 and 9 (shell); ©Shutterstock / Joanne Harris & Daniel Bubrick: p.8 and 9 ('a' magnet); ©Shutterstock / Marcus Miranda: p.8 and 9 (6 magnet); ©Shutterstock / Serg64: p.8 and 9 (nut); ©Shutterstock / Trinacria Photo: p.8 and 9 (badge): ©Shutterstock / optimarc: p.8 and 9 (die); ©Shutterstock / Sergey Vasilyev: p. 8 and 9 (marble); ©Shutterstock / Janny Jus: p.8 and 9 (walnut); ©Shutterstock / Jiri Vaclavek: p.13 (spider); ©Alamy / D. Hurst: p.13 (octopus); ©Shutterstock / Ivonne Wierink: p.13 (cat); ©Pearson Education / Tudor Photography: p.13 (dinosaur); ©Shutterstock / Pashka: p.13 (monkey); ©Shutterstock / Francseco Abrignani: page 34 (cards);
All other photos © Pearson Education / Clark Wiseman, Studio 8.

Every effort has been made to contact copyright holders of material reproduced in this book. Any omissions will be rectified in subsequent printings if notice is given to the publishers.

Websites
The websites used in this book were correct and up-to-date at the time of publication. It is essential for tutors to preview each website before using it in class so as to ensure that the URL is still accurate, relevant and appropriate. We suggest that tutors bookmark useful websites and consider enabling students to access them through the school/college intranet.

Contents

Using this book

Your teacher will talk to you about where you will start in *Rapid Maths*.

Welcome to *Rapid Maths*.

Getting started

Check that you can do the first two pages in each part of this book, before you do any more.

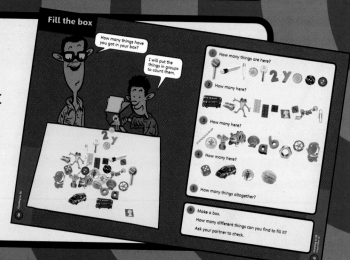

Reading

There are word lists in the Teacher's Guide.

These will help you learn any new words you need.

I've made cards from my list.

Extra activities

There are more activities and games in the Copymasters, Games Pack and Home Maths Book.

There is Practice Software too, with activities for each level of *Rapid Maths*.

Take them home for extra practice!

We like doing the Speedy Sums!

Can we get more right, and get quicker?

Progress tests and Record sheets

These are in the Teacher's Guide.

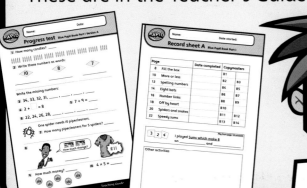

Check on your progress…

and keep a record of what you've done!

Part I
Contents

■ Counting and place value

■ Addition and subtraction

■ Multiplication and division

How many things have you got in your box?

I will put the things in groups to count them.

1 How many things are here?

2 How many here?

3 How many here?

4 How many here?

5 How many things altogether?

6 Make a box.

How many different things can you find to fill it?

Ask your partner to check.

More or less

I'm counting forwards.
1, 2, 3, 4, 5, ...

I'm counting backwards.
12, 11, 10, 9, 8, ...

Copy these. Write the next four numbers.

1   9, 10, 11, 12, ...

2   10, 9, 8, 7, ...

3   20, 21, 22, 23, ...

4   15, 14, 13, 12, ...

5   23, 24, 25, 26, ...

6   30, 29, 28, 27, ...

7   23, 22, 21, 20, ...

8   17, 16, 15, 14, ...

9   35, 36, 37, 38, ...

10   38, 39, 40, 41, ...

11 What is one more than 13?

12 What is one more than 19?

13 What is one more than 37?

14 What is one more than 48?

15 What is one less than 16?

16 What is one less than 34?

Spelling numbers

Which numbers can you spell?

1 one	2 two	3 three	4 four	5 five

Do these sums. Write the answers as words.

1. Four add one
2. Three add one
3. One add two
4. One add one
5. Two add two
6. Three add two
7. Two add one
8. Two add three

6 six	7 seven	8 eight	9 nine	10 ten

9. Four add four
10. Five add five
11. Three add four
12. Six add three
13. Three add three
14. Six add two
15. Seven add two
16. Six add one

Write the answers as words.

17 How many legs?

21 How many legs?

18 How many legs?

22 How many legs?

19 How many legs?

23 How many legs?

20 How many legs?

24 How many legs?

Eight bats

Count the bats.

8 bats are sleeping.

No bats are flying.

$8 + 0 = 8$

1 How many are sleeping?

2 How many are flying?

3

$7 + 1 =$

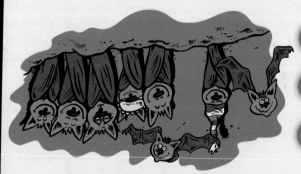

4 How many are sleeping?

5 How many are flying?

6

$6 + 2 =$

7 How many are sleeping?

8 How many are flying?

9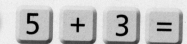

$5 + 3 =$

Addition bonds to 8

10 How many are sleeping?

11 How many are flying?

12 | 4 | + | 4 | = |

13 How many are sleeping?

14 How many are flying?

15 | 3 | + | 5 | = |

16 How many are sleeping?

17 How many are flying?

18 | 2 | + | 6 | = |

19 How many are sleeping?

20 How many are flying?

21 | 1 | + | 7 | = |

22

No bats are sleeping.
How many are flying?

Number links

Here are 7 bricks.

4 red
3 yellow

What sums can you do with them?

1

4 + 3 =

2

3 + 4 =

3

7 – 3 =

4

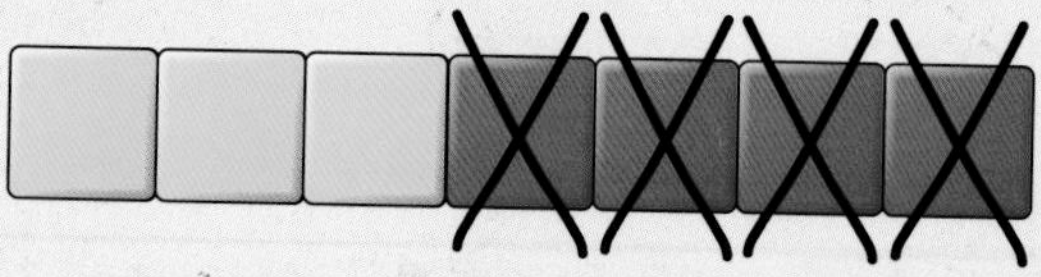

7 – 4 =

The numbers are linked. **3 4 7**

Use bricks.

   1 5 6

5 1 + 5

6 5 + 1

7 6 – 1

8 6 – 5

Links between addition and subtraction

2   5   7

9   2 + 5

10   5 + 2

11   7 − 2

12   7 − 5

3   2   5

13   3 + 2

14   2 + 3

15   5 − 3

16   5 − 2

3   3   6

17   3 + 3

18   6 − 3

I can only make two sums because two numbers are the same.

4   4   8

19   4 + 4

20   8 − 4

Links between addition and subtraction
Copymasters B8 and B9

Off by heart

Which sums do you know off by heart?

**2 add 2 makes 4
1 add 2 makes 3**

**If you do a sum lots of times,
you can learn the answer off by heart.**

Copy and complete.

Ring any sums you know off by heart.

Off by heart

1. (2 + 1 = 3)

2. 1 + 3 =

1	2 + 1 =		5	1 + 2 =		9	2 + 3 =
2	1 + 3 =		6	4 + 0 =		10	4 + 1 =
3	0 + 5 =		7	2 + 2 =		11	1 + 4 =
4	3 + 0 =		8	3 + 1 =		12	3 + 2 =

Now try with bigger numbers.

13 1 + 5 =

14 2 + 4 =

15 5 + 1 =

16 4 + 2 =

17 3 + 3 =

18 6 + 1 =

19 1 + 6 =

20 3 + 4 =

21 4 + 3 =

22 2 + 5 =

23 6 + 0 =

24 5 + 2 =

Do these sums make 7? Write Yes or No.

25 5 + 2 =

26 4 + 3 =

27 2 + 6 =

28 3 + 4 =

29 4 + 1 =

30 6 + 1 =

Do these sums make 8? Write Yes or No.

31 4 + 4 =

32 3 + 5 =

33 2 + 6 =

34 8 + 0 =

Ask if you can play the 'Sums which make 8' game.

Mental recall of addition within 8
Copymaster B10
The 'Sums which make 8' game (B26, B27 and B28)

19

You can make a spider with ten pipecleaners.

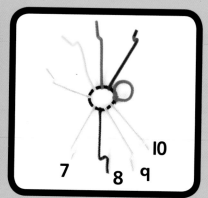

How many pipecleaners for:

1 two spiders?

2 three spiders?

3 four spiders?

4 five spiders?

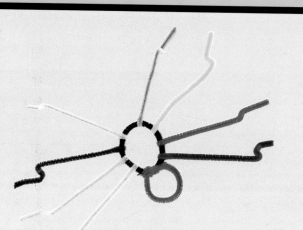

How many spiders can you make with:

5 30 pipecleaners?

6 20 pipecleaners?

7 50 pipecleaners?

8 40 pipecleaners?

9 How many pipecleaners?

You can make a snake with two pipecleaners.

10 How many pipecleaners?

How many pipecleaners?

11

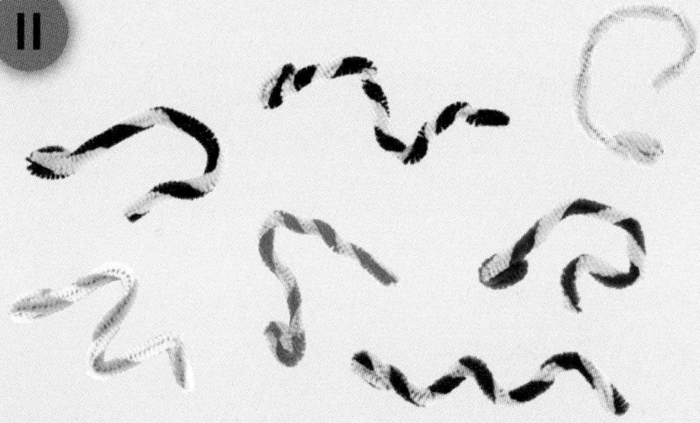

12

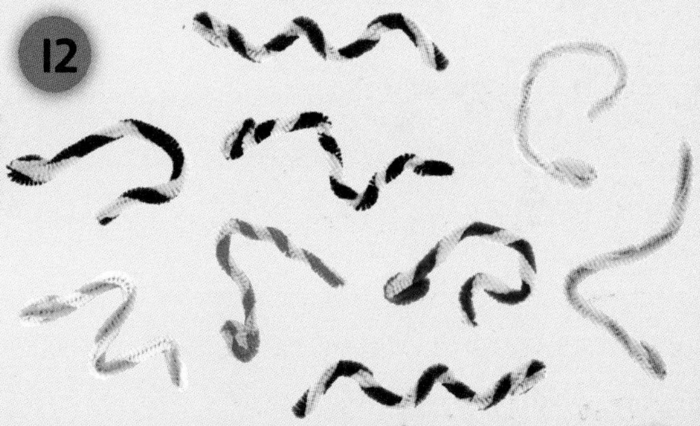

How many snakes can you make with:

13 20 pipecleaners?

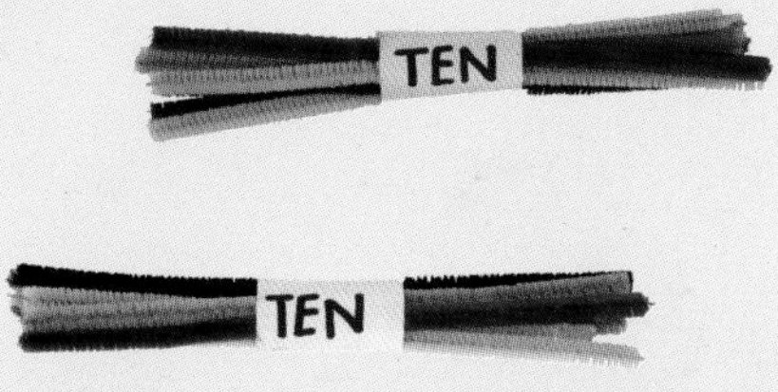

TEN

TEN

14 30 pipecleaners?

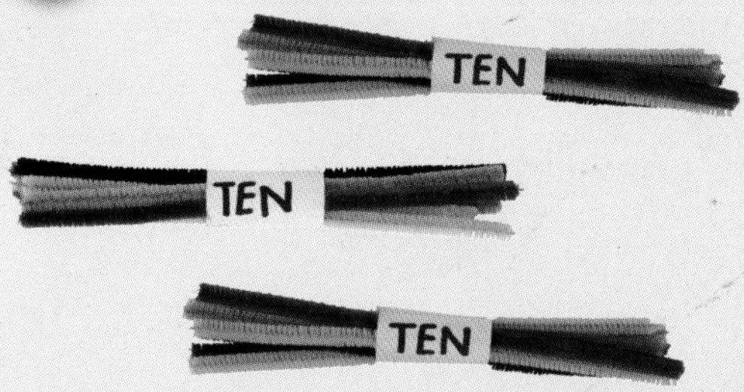

TEN

TEN

TEN

Speedy sums

Can you get 10 sums right in 3 minutes?

Use a stopwatch or a sand timer.

1	2 + 4 =	6	1 + 4 =
2	1 + 7 =	7	3 + 3 =
3	5 + 3 =	8	6 + 2 =
4	4 + 0 =	9	4 + 3 =
5	2 + 2 =	10	0 + 3 =

Check your answers. ✔ or ✘

How many of these sums can you get right in 3 minutes?

1	7 – 2 =	6	3 – 1 =
2	4 – 1 =	7	4 – 3 =
3	8 – 4 =	8	2 – 2 =
4	5 – 3 =	9	7 – 4 =
5	6 – 5 =	10	6 – 2 =

✔ or ✘

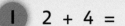

How many can you get right in 3 minutes?

1	4 + 2 =	6	5 – 1 =
2	6 – 4 =	7	3 + 5 =
3	7 + 0 =	8	7 – 3 =
4	4 – 2 =	9	6 + 1 =
5	1 + 5 =	10	3 – 3 =

Use Speedy Sums A made from Copymaster B13.

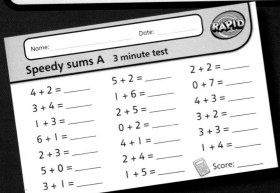

RAPID

Name: _____ Date: _____

Speedy sums A   3 minute test

4 + 2 = _____
3 + 4 = _____
1 + 3 = _____
6 + 1 = _____
2 + 3 = _____
5 + 0 = _____
3 + 1 = _____

5 + 2 = _____
1 + 6 = _____
2 + 5 = _____
0 + 2 = _____
4 + 1 = _____
2 + 4 = _____
1 + 5 = _____

2 + 2 = _____
0 + 7 = _____
4 + 3 = _____
3 + 2 = _____
3 + 3 = _____
1 + 4 = _____

Score: _____

Can you get 20 sums right in 3 minutes?

Check your answers. ✔ or ✘
Count how many you got right.

Ask what to do next.

T-shirts

How much change?

You can count up...

£6   +   £4 = £10

or take away.

$$10 - 6 = 4$$

So there is £4 change.

1

How much change?

2 How much change?

3

How much change?

red £5 each

green £6 each

white £3 each

I bought two green t-shirts.

4 How much did I spend?

5  How much change?

I bought a red t-shirt and two white ones.

6 How much did I spend?

7 How much change?

I bought a green t-shirt and a white one.

8 How much did I spend?

9 How much change?

10

What could I buy with £10?

Addition and subtraction within 20
Copymaster B17

Bowling

There are 10 skittles.

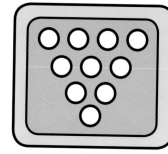

From above they looked like this.

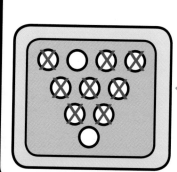

I knocked down 8 skittles. That's 2 still standing.

1. Emma knocked down 3 skittles.

   How many still standing?

2. Li knocked down 5 skittles.

   How many still standing?

3. Maya knocked down 9 skittles.

   How many still standing?

4   Max knocked down 6 skittles.

How many still standing?

5   Max's Dad knocked down 1 skittle.

How many still standing?

6   Emma knocked down 4 skittles.

How many still standing?

7   Li knocked down 2 skittles.

How many still standing?

8   Maya knocked down 10 skittles.

How many still standing?

q   Max knocked down 7 skittles.

How many still standing?

10   Max's Dad didn't knock down any skittles.

How many still standing?

Fives and ones

This is 5p...

and this is 5p.

How much money is in each box?

1

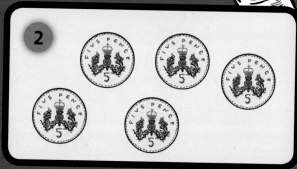

2

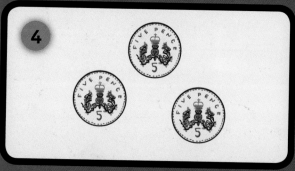

3

4

5

You need: 35p in 5p coins and 4p in 1p coins.

Make each amount with coins.

Draw it neatly.

Or print it, with coin stamps.

6	10p	11	18p	16	30p
7	7p	12	14p	17	29p
8	9p	13	20p	18	33p
9	16p	14	22p	19	35p
10	13p	15	27p	20	38p

Ask if you can play the 'Fifty pence' game.

Counting in 5s to 50
Copymasters B18 and B19
The 'Fifty Pence' game (B29 and B30)

G

Pick up bricks

Jack picked up these bricks with one hand.

1 How many bricks?

I put the bricks in tens. It's easier to count them.

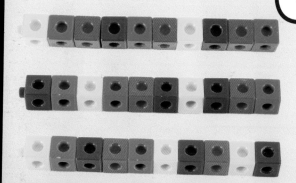

2 How many bricks?

How many bricks?

3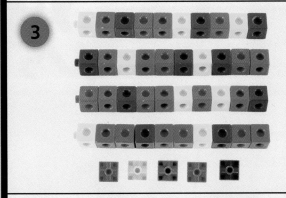

5

4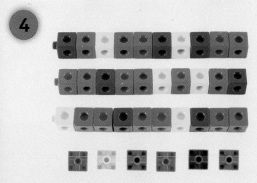

6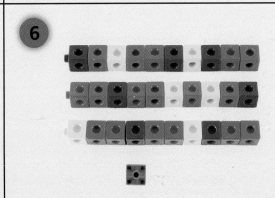

7

Pick up some bricks with one hand.

Count them in ones.

Put them in tens and count again.

Write how many you picked up.

Have three turns.

Bat and fives

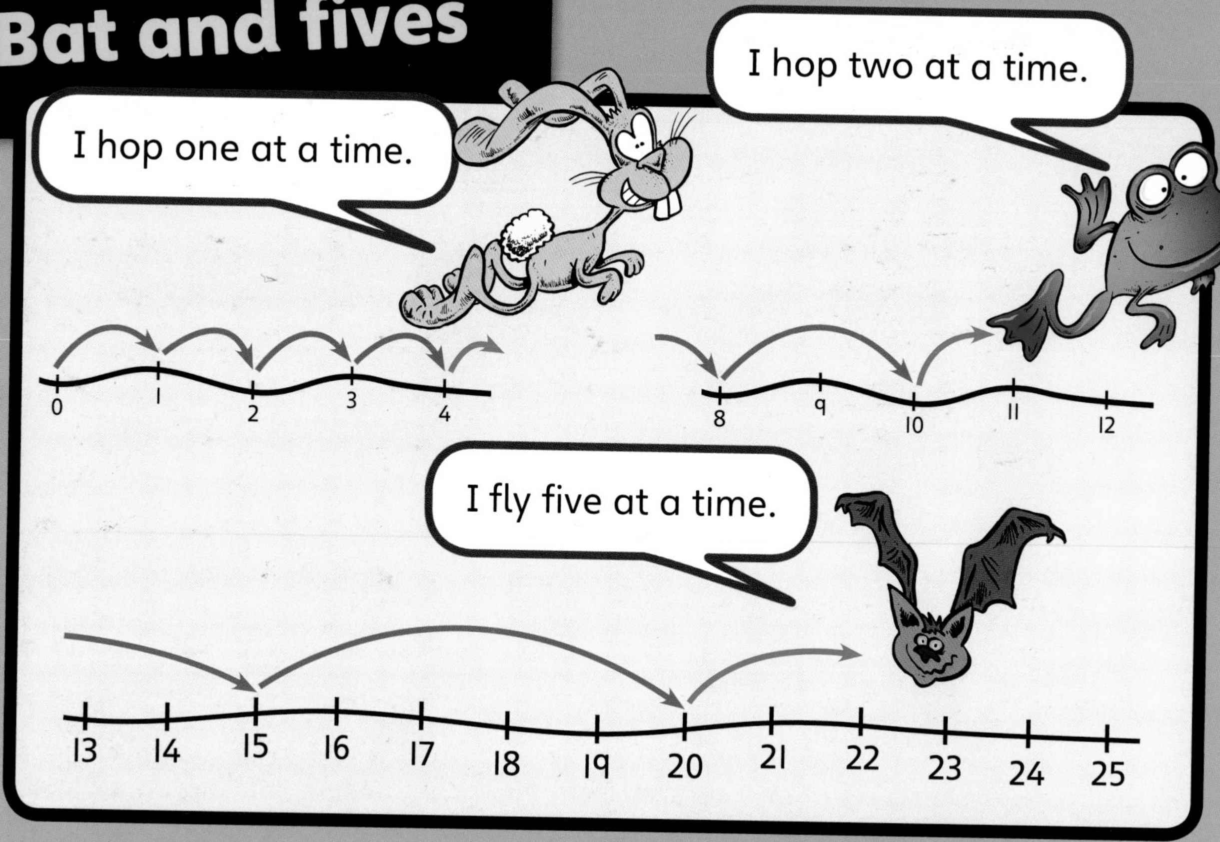
I hop one at a time.
0 1 2 3 4
I hop two at a time.
8 9 10 11 12
I fly five at a time.
13 14 15 16 17 18 19 20 21 22 23 24 25

Which number will the bat land on next?

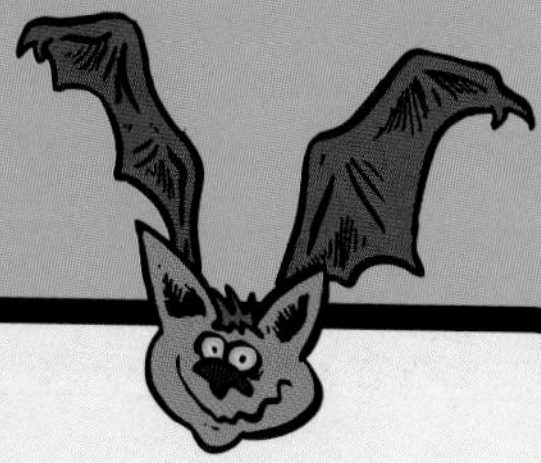

1

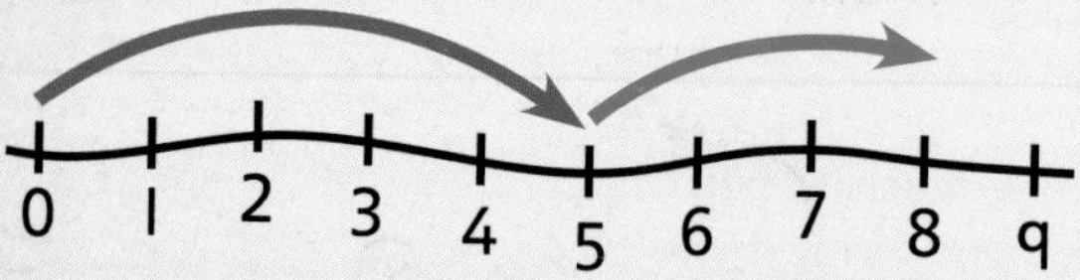
0 1 2 3 4 5 6 7 8 9

4

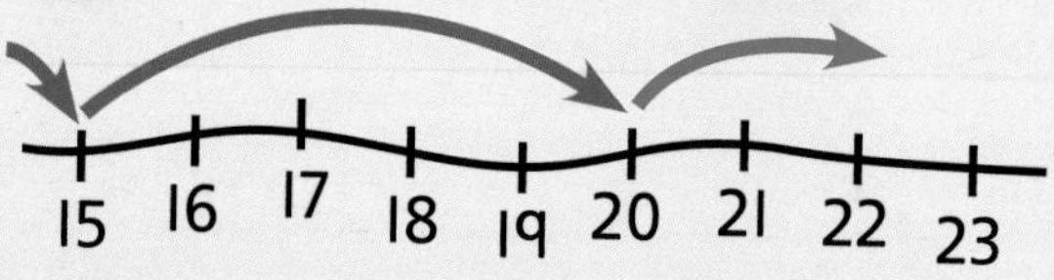
15 16 17 18 19 20 21 22 23

2

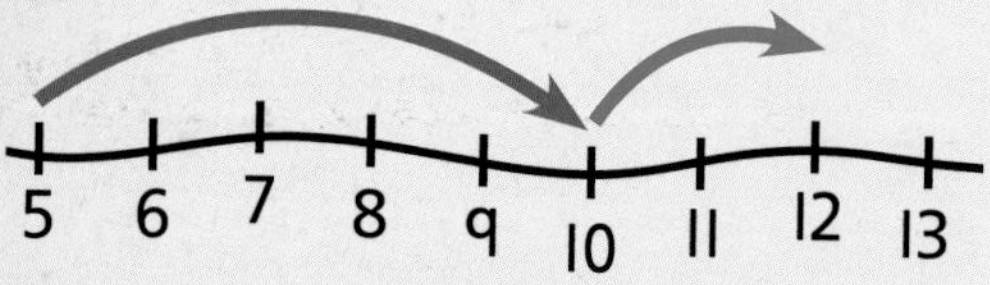
5 6 7 8 9 10 11 12 13

5

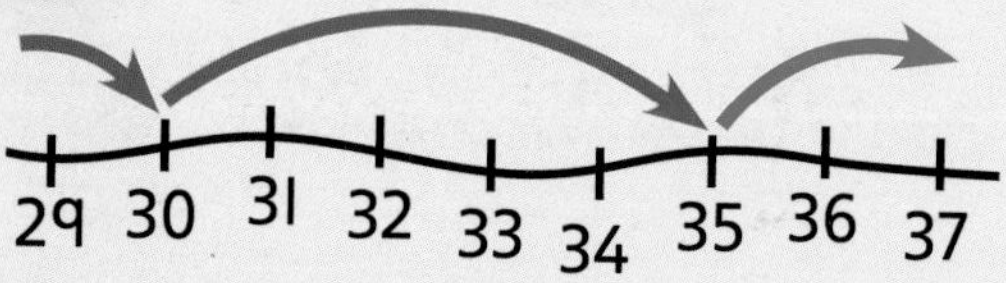
29 30 31 32 33 34 35 36 37

3

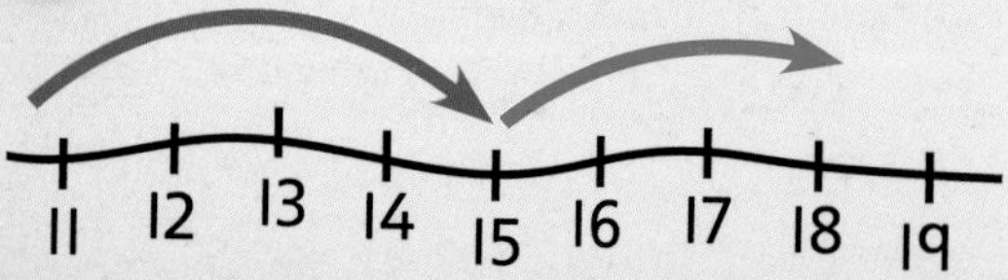
11 12 13 14 15 16 17 18 19

6

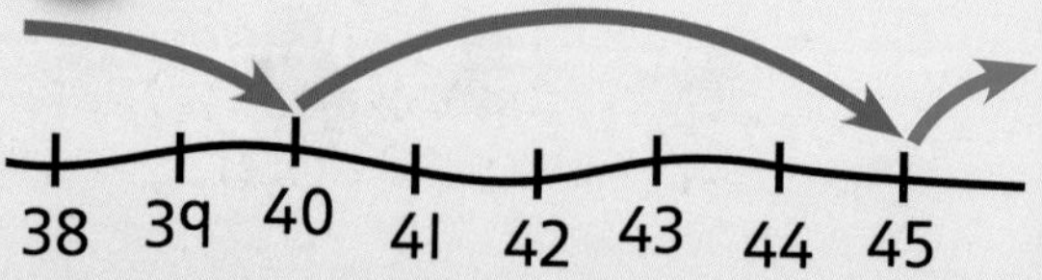
38 39 40 41 42 43 44 45

0, 5, 10, 15, 20, 25, 30, …

… 35, 40, 45, 50, …
These numbers are called
<u>multiples of five</u>.

You can get <u>multiples of five</u>
by adding fives,
or by <u>multiplying</u> by five.

Use a calculator.

Look for this button: $\times$

7 5 $+$ 5 $+$ 5 $=$

That's 3 fives.
3 times 5

8 3 $\times$ 5 $=$

9 5 $+$ 5 $+$ 5 $+$ 5 $=$

10 4 $\times$ 5 $=$

I practise adding with playing cards.

I pick two cards and add them.

Check

q + 3 = 12

Add these.

1

4

This counts as 1.

2

5

3

6

Red and black

A game for 2 people.

Shuffle the red cards.
Put them in a pile, face down.
Shuffle the black cards.
Put them in a pile, face down.

Take a red card
and a black card.
Add them.

You need:
- a pack of playing cards,
  <u>without</u> the picture cards
- a calculator

Your partner can check
with a calculator.

If you are right, keep the cards.
If not, put them back at the
bottom of each pile.

Now it's your partner's go.

Keep going until all the cards have gone.

Work with a partner if you want to.

You need 20 playing cards.

Find as many ways as you can to make 12, with a red card and a black card.

Draw or write down each way.

Part 2
Contents

Counting and place value

Addition and subtraction

Multiplication and division

I save pennies.
I put them in piles of ten to count.

There is 34p here.

How much money?

 1
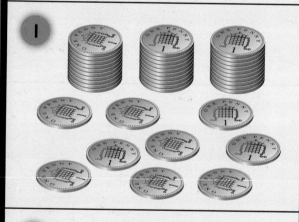

3

2
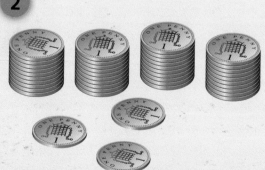

4

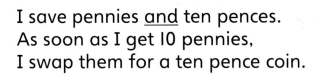

I save pennies <u>and</u> ten pences.
As soon as I get 10 pennies,
I swap them for a ten pence coin.

How much money?

5

7

6

8

Ask if you can play the 'Sixty pence' game.

Counting to 60
Copymaster B31
The 'Sixty pence' game (B56 and B57)

G

Sums in words

Use sums to practise your spelling.

1 Copy these.

| **11** eleven | **12** twelve | **13** thirteen | **14** fourteen | **15** fifteen |

Do these. Write the answers as words.

2 Ten add one

3 Ten add four

4 Ten add five

5 Six add six

6 Eight add five

7 Nine add two

8 Seven add seven

9 Ten add three

10 Eleven add one

11 Thirteen add two

12 Four add ten

13 Nine add three

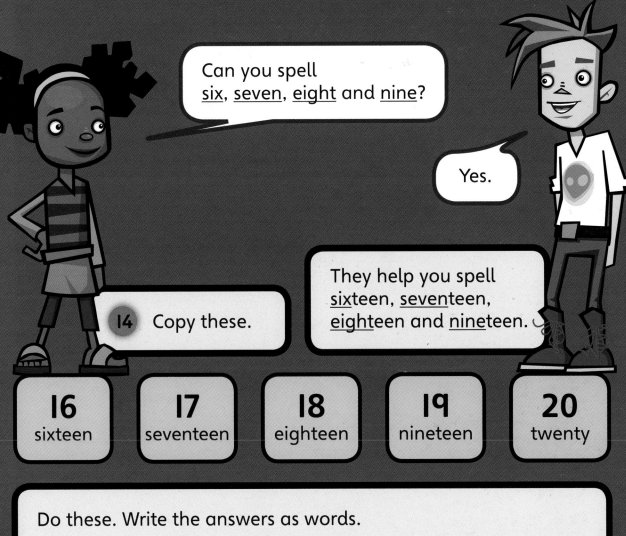

Can you spell
<u>six</u>, <u>seven</u>, <u>eight</u> and <u>nine</u>?

Yes.

14 Copy these.

They help you spell
<u>six</u>teen, <u>seven</u>teen,
<u>eigh</u>teen and <u>nine</u>teen.

| 16 sixteen | 17 seventeen | 18 eighteen | 19 nineteen | 20 twenty |

Do these. Write the answers as words.

15 Eight add ten

16 Six add ten

17 Ten add ten

18 Eighteen add one

19 Seven add ten

20 Twelve add four

21 Nine add ten

22 Sixteen add one

23 Seventeen add one

24

Fifteen add five

These tens and ones help us learn about numbers.

You can make a number with ones …

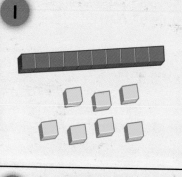

24

or tens and ones.

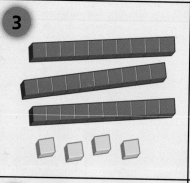

24

How many?

1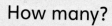

3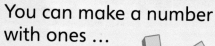

5

2

4

6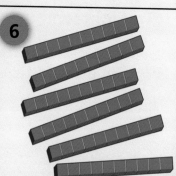

Work with a partner.

I'll check your number.

Yes, that's 23.

Make each number with tens and ones.

Then draw it.

(23)

7	12	10	37	13	41	16	17
8	43	11	50	14	35	17	36
9	26	12	59	15	28	18	54

Ask if you can play the 'Tens and ones' game.

Counting in 10s and 1s to 60
Copymasters B34 and B35
The 'Tens and ones' game (B58 and B59)

G

43

0, 2, 4, 6, 8, 10, 12, …

These numbers are called <u>multiples of two</u>.

You can get <u>multiples of two</u> by adding twos, or by <u>multiplying</u> by two.

One bird

1 How many legs?

2 $\boxed{1} \times \boxed{2} =$

Three birds

6 How many legs?

7 2 + 2 + 2

8 $\boxed{3} \times \boxed{2} =$

Two birds

3 How many legs?

4 2 + 2

5 $\boxed{2} \times \boxed{2} =$

Four birds

9 How many legs?

10 2 + 2 + 2 + 2

11 $\boxed{4} \times \boxed{2} =$

Five birds

12 How many legs?

13 2 + 2 + 2 + 2 + 2

14 | 5 | × | 2 | = |

Seven birds

18 How many legs?

19 2 + 2 + 2 + 2 + 2 + 2 + 2

20 | 7 | × | 2 | = |

Six birds

15 How many legs?

16 2 + 2 + 2 + 2 + 2 + 2

17 | 6 | × | 2 | = |

Sixteen legs!

21 How many birds?

22 2 + 2 + 2 + 2 + 2 + 2 + 2 + 2

23 | 8 | × | 2 | = |

24 Copy and complete.

Two times table

$0 × 2 =$ $4 × 2 =$ $8 × 2 =$

$1 × 2 =$ $5 × 2 =$ $9 × 2 =$

$2 × 2 =$ $6 × 2 =$ $10 × 2 =$

$3 × 2 =$ $7 × 2 =$

I dropped my clock! The big hand fell off.

You can still use it to tell the time for hours and half hours.

Does the clock say 2 o'clock? Write <u>Yes</u> or <u>No</u>.

1

2

3

What's the time?

4 o'clock

What is the time?

4

5

6

What's the time?

This hand is halfway between the 3 and the 4.

It is half past 3.

What is the time?

7

9

11

8

10

12

Use a real clock (with two hands!)

13 Make the clock say 3 o'clock. Draw it.

14 Make the clock say half past 3. Draw it.

Using halves: telling the time
Copymasters B38 and B39

No red counters. q yellow counters.

$$0 + q = q$$

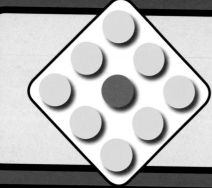

1. How many red counters?

2. How many yellow counters?

3. $1 + 8 =$

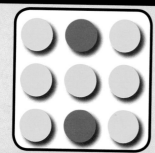

4. How many red?

5. How many yellow?

6. $2 + 7 =$

7. How many red?

8. How many yellow?

q. $3 + 6 =$

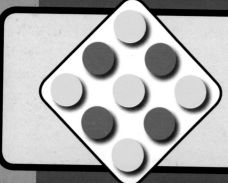

10. How many red?

11. How many yellow?

12. $4 + 5 =$

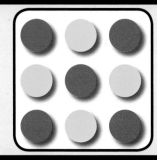

13 How many red counters?

14 How many yellow counters?

15 $5 + 4 =$

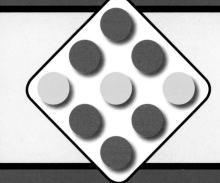

16 How many red?

17 How many yellow?

18 $6 + 3 =$

19 How many red?

20 How many yellow?

21 $7 + 2 =$

22 How many red?

23 How many yellow?

24 $8 + 1 =$

Ask if you can play the 'Make 9' game.

Ⓖ

Addition bonds to 9
Copymasters B40 and B41.
The 'Make 9' game (B60 and B61)

49

This is 10p ...

and this is 10p.

How much money is in each box?

1

2

3

4

You can swap 4 fives …

for 2 tens.

5 6 fives … How many tens?

6 8 fives … How many tens?

7 10 fives … How many tens?

8 One ten … How many fives?

9 5 tens … How many fives?

10 How can you make 50p with fives and tens?

Draw all the ways.

Here's one way.

You can do sums quickly
if you learn them off by heart.

Speedy sums

1. (2 + 2 = 4)

2. 4 + 1 =

Copy and complete.
Ring any sums
you know off by heart.

1	2 + 2 =	5	6 + 1 =	9	3 + 2 =
2	4 + 1 =	6	4 + 4 =	10	0 + 1 =
3	5 + 2 =	7	1 + 3 =	11	1 + 1 =
4	3 + 3 =	8	1 + 6 =	12	0 + 2 =

13	2 + 4 =	17	1 + 2 =
14	2 + 1 =	18	5 + 1 =
15	4 + 0 =	19	3 + 0 =
16	2 + 3 =	20	3 + 4 =

✔ or ✗

Do these make 8?
Write <u>Yes</u> or <u>No</u>.

21 4 + 4

22 5 + 2

23 0 + 8

24 3 + 6

25 1 + 6

26 2 + 6

Do these make 5?
Write <u>Yes</u> or <u>No</u>.

27 6 – 1

28 9 – 4

29 8 – 0

30 8 – 3

31 7 – 3

32 6 – 2

33 5 – 0

34 5 – 5

35 9 – 2

 Use a stopwatch or a sand timer.

Can you get 20 sums right in 3 minutes?

Use Speedy Sums E made from Copymaster B44.

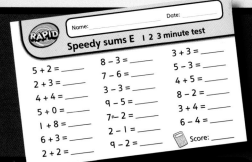

RAPID

Name: _____ Date: _____

Speedy sums E 1 2 3 minute test

5 + 2 = _____	8 – 3 = _____	3 + 3 = _____
2 + 3 = _____	7 – 6 = _____	5 – 3 = _____
4 + 4 = _____	3 – 3 = _____	4 + 5 = _____
5 + 0 = _____	9 – 5 = _____	8 – 2 = _____
1 + 8 = _____	7 – 2 = _____	3 + 4 = _____
6 + 3 = _____	2 – 1 = _____	6 – 4 = _____
2 + 2 = _____	9 – 2 = _____	Score: _____

Check your answers. ✔ or ✘
Count how many you got right.

Ask what to do next.

Boxes

Sunesh and Emma are playing 'Boxes'.

We take turns to draw a line.

If my line makes a box, I put my letter in it ... and draw another line.

1st game

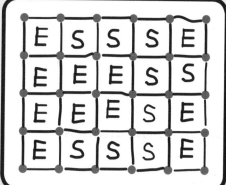

Emma got 11 boxes.
Sunesh got 9.

1. Who won, Emma or Sunesh?

2. How many boxes altogether?

$$11 + 9 =$$

2nd game

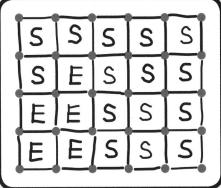

(3) How many boxes for Emma?

(4) How many for Sunesh?

(5) How many boxes altogether?

(6) Who won?

3rd game

I got 10 boxes.

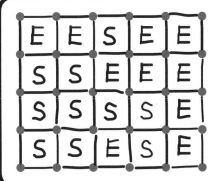

No, that's not right.
I got 11 boxes.
11 + 10 does <u>not</u> make 20.

(7) How many boxes for Emma?

(8) How many for Sunesh?

(9) How many boxes altogether?

(10) Who won?

4th game

I got 12 boxes.

(11) How many for Sunesh?

(12) Who won?

Addition to 20
Copymasters B45 and B46

Teen numbers

Thirteen

$$10 + 3 = 13$$

Make each number with a ten and ones.

Copy and complete.

Fourteen	**1** $10 + 4 =$ **2** $4 + 10 =$
Nineteen	**3** $10 + 9 =$ **4** $9 + 10 =$
Sixteen	**5** $10 + 6 =$ **6** $6 + 10 =$
Fifteen	**7** $10 + 5 =$ **8** $5 + 10 =$
Eighteen	**9** $10 + 8 =$ **10** $8 + 10 =$

✔ or ✗

I like using ones to add up.

I like using tens and ones. It's quicker.

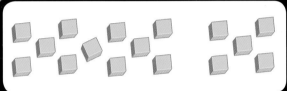

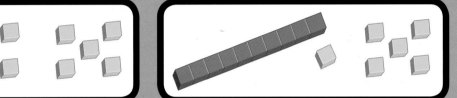

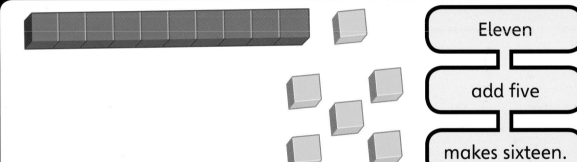

Eleven

add five

makes sixteen.

Use tens and ones. Copy and complete.

11 15 + 2 =

12 10 + 4 =

13 12 + 6 =

14 11 + 4 =

15 14 + 3 =

16 11 + 6 =

17 13 + 2 =

18 12 + 4 =

Five times table

0, 5, 10, 15, 20, 25, ...

These numbers are called <u>multiples of five</u>.

You can get <u>multiples of five</u> by adding fives, or by <u>multiplying</u> by five.

One starfish

1 How many legs?

2 | 1 | × | 5 | = |

Three starfish

6 How many legs?

7 5 + 5 + 5

8 | 3 | × | 5 | = |

Two starfish

3 How many legs?

4 5 + 5

5 | 2 | × | 5 | = |

Four starfish

9 How many legs?

10 5 + 5 + 5 + 5

11 | 4 | × | 5 | = |

Five starfish

12 How many legs?

13 5 + 5 + 5 + 5 + 5

14 5 × 5 =

Seven starfish

18 How many legs?

19 5 + 5 + 5 + 5 + 5 + 5 + 5

20 7 × 5 =

Six starfish

15 How many legs?

16 5 + 5 + 5 + 5 + 5 + 5

17 6 × 5 =

Eight starfish behind a rock.

21 How many legs?

22 5 + 5 + 5 + 5 + 5 + 5 + 5 + 5

23 8 × 5 =

24 Copy and complete.

Five times table

0 × 5 =	4 × 5 =	8 × 5 =
1 × 5 =	5 × 5 =	9 × 5 =
2 × 5 =	6 × 5 =	10 × 5 =
3 × 5 =	7 × 5 =	

What's sixteen take away ten?

Six

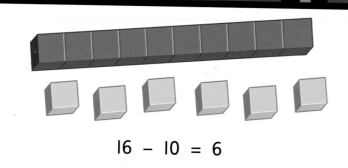

$16 - 10 = 6$

Make each number with a ten and ones.

Copy and complete.

Fifteen	**1**	$15 - 10 =$
	2	$15 - 5 =$
Thirteen	**3**	$13 - 10 =$
	4	$13 - 3 =$
Seventeen	**5**	$17 - 10 =$
	6	$17 - 7 =$
Nineteen	**7**	$19 - 10 =$
	8	$19 - 9 =$

✔ or ✗

Eighteen take away four is fourteen.

You can draw it, if you want to.

$18 - 4 = 14$

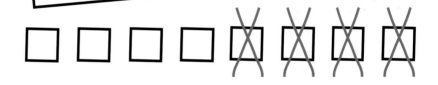

Use tens and ones. Copy and complete.

9 $18 - 3 =$

10 $14 - 10 =$

11 $17 - 6 =$

12 $15 - 5 =$

13 $19 - 7 =$

14 $13 - 2 =$

15 $16 - 1 =$

16 $18 - 11 =$

✔ or ✗

Photos

I can take 24 photos with this camera.

1 I've taken 2 photos. How many more can I take?

2 Now I've taken 4 photos. How many more can I take?

3 Now I've taken 12 photos. How many more can I take?

4 Now I've taken 17 photos. How many more can I take?

5 Now I've taken 20 photos. How many more can I take?

6 Now I've taken 24 photos. How many more can I take?

You took 14 photos of your cat, 2 photos of your finger, and 8 photos of me!

7 Check the total.   14 + 2 + 8

8 These all make 24.

$$14 + 2 + 8 = 24$$
$$12 + 12 = 24$$
$$20 + 4 = 24$$
$$10 + 10 + 4 = 24$$

Write ten more sums that make 24.

Ask a friend to check.   ✔ or ✗

Hopping frogs

We score 3 points for each frog in the dish.

3 + 3 + 3 = 9

9 points

What did we score?

1

2 frogs in the dish.

3 + 3 = ___

2 4 frogs in the dish.

3 5 frogs in the dish.

What did we score?

4 None in.

5 6 frogs in the dish.

6 I scored 12 points.

How many frogs in the dish?

7 Emma scored 3. How many frogs in the dish?

8 Li scored 9. How many frogs in the dish?

9 Maya scored 15. How many frogs in the dish?

10 John scored 6. How many frogs in the dish?

Work with a partner if you want to.
Make a £10 note and three £5 notes.
Collect fifteen '£1 coins'.

   or

Find as many ways as you can to make £15.

Draw each way.

This is one way.

Part 3
Contents

Counting and place value

Addition and subtraction

Multiplication and division

Mixed problems

Joke Shop

Can you find the joke biscuit?

1   How many biscuits altogether?

I bought a packet of joke ants!

2 How many ants altogether?

Tens and teens

Use sums to practise your spelling.

1 Copy these.

| 30 thirty | 40 forty | 50 fifty | 60 sixty | 70 seventy |

Do these. Write the answers as words.

2 Twenty add ten

3 Forty add ten

4 Thirty add ten

5 Forty add twenty

6 Ten add twenty

7 Ten add sixty

8 Thirty add twenty

9 Fifty add twenty

10 Thirty add thirty

11 Twenty add twenty

12 Ten add ten add ten

13 Fifty add ten

4	**4th**	**14**	**40**
four	fourth	fourteen	forty

Forty does not have a u.

Write these numbers as words.

14 **4**   15 **14**   16 **40**   17 **4th**

When you say **13** and **30** the first part sounds the same.

Work with a partner.
Say these out loud, then write the numbers as words.

18 **17** and **70**   21 **16** and **60**

19 **15** and **50**   22 **13** and **30**

20 **14** and **40**

Ask if you can play 'Tens and teens bingo'.

2, 4, 6, 8, 10, 12, …

You're counting in twos.

Copy these. Write the next three numbers.

1 10, 12, 14, 16, …

2 16, 14, 12, 10, …

3 22, 24, 26, 28, …

4 26, 28, 30, 32, …

5 30, 28, 26, 24, …

6 38, 40, 42, 44, …

7 40, 38, 36, 34, …

8 16, 18, 20, 22, …

0 1 2 3 4 5 6 7 8 9 10 11 12 13 14 15 16 17 18

The red numbers are called <u>even</u> numbers.

9 What are the blue numbers called?

I'm counting in fives.
5, 10, 15, 20, 25, …

Copy these. Write the next three numbers.

10   5, 10, 15, 20, …

11   50, 45, 40, 35, …

12

What am I counting in?
10, 20, 30, 40, 50, 60, …

Counting backwards is harder than counting forwards.

Practise with a partner.

<u>Count out loud</u> from 20 down to 0 in twos.
Your partner can check.

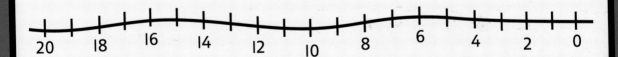

20   18   16   14   12   10   8   6   4   2   0

<u>Count out loud</u> from 50 down to 0 in fives.
Your partner can check.

50   45   40   35   30   25   20   15   10   5   0

Multiples of 2, 5 and 10
Copymasters B65 and B66

Footballs

£9, please.

1   How much change?

Copy and complete.

2   10 − 9 =

3   9 + ☐ = 10

£8, please.

4   How much change?

5   10 − 8 =

6   8 + ☐ = 10

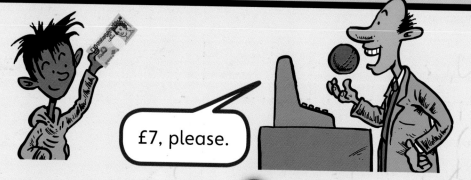

£7, please.

7   How much change?

8   10 − 7 =

9   7 + ☐ = 10

£6, please.

Copy and complete.

10 How much change?

11 10 – 6 =

12 6 + ☐ = 10

£5, please.

13 How much change?

14 10 – 5 =

15 5 + ☐ = 10

Copy and complete.

16 10 – 4 =

17 4 + ☐ = 10

18 10 – 3 =

19 3 + ☐ = 10

20 10 – 2 =

21 2 + ☐ = 10

22 10 – 1 =

23 1 + ☐ = 10

Ask if you can play the 'Sums which make 10' game.

G

Addition and subtraction bonds to 10
Copymasters B67 and B68. 'The Sums which
make 10' game (B90, B91 and B92)

Easier adding

You can add up in any order.

Copy and complete.

1	8 + 2 =	3	2 + 13 =	5	15 + 4 =
2	2 + 8 =	4	13 + 2 =	6	4 + 15 =

I put the bigger number first ...

because I think it's easier.

I do this ...

11 + 3

11... add 3... makes 14

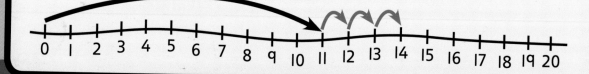

not this ...

3 + 11

3... add 11.................................. makes 14

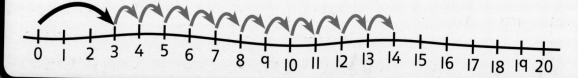

Which way do <u>you</u> think is easier? Talk to your partner about it.

0	1 2 3 4 5 6 7 8 9 10 11 12 13 14 15 16 17 18 19 20					

Put the biggest number first.
Use the number line if you want to.

7 4 + 12	**11** 1 + 16	**15** 1 + 12 + 1
8 3 + 16	**12** 9 + 4	**16** 5 + 2 + 9
9 12 + 7	**13** 2 + 4 + 13	**17** 4 + 1 + 8
10 8 + 9	**14** 7 + 9 + 2	**18** 1 + 14 + 5

Sometimes you can find <u>tens</u> when you add up three numbers.

8 + 7 + 2

8 add 2 makes 10.
10 add 7 makes 17.

Look for tens. Copy and complete.

19 5 + 4 + 5	**21** 4 + 13 + 6	**23** 2 + 9 + 8
20 6 + 1 + 9	**22** 4 + 9 + 6	**24** 7 + 4 + 6

Addition within 30
Copymasters B69 and B70

Speedy sums

Work with a partner.

Write question numbers 1 to 20.
Ask your partner to read the
questions to you.

Write your answers
as quickly as you can.

1	2 + 8	8	7 − 1	15	1 + 5
2	0 + 4	9	10 − 4	16	8 − 6
3	6 + 3	10	3 − 0	17	4 + 4
4	5 + 5	11	6 − 3	18	10 − 3
5	2 + 5	12	7 − 4	19	7 + 2
6	1 + 9	13	4 − 2	20	9 − 8
7	3 + 5	14	9 − 4		

✔ or ✘

Now <u>you</u> read the questions
to your partner.

Do these make 10?
Write <u>Yes</u> or <u>No</u>.

21	0 + 10	**23**	3 + 7	**25**	8 + 1
22	2 + 7	**24**	5 + 5	**26**	6 + 4

Do these make 7?
Write <u>Yes</u> or <u>No</u>.

27	3 + 4	**30**	9 − 2	**33**	8 − 2
28	6 + 2	**31**	1 + 6	**34**	7 − 0
29	10 − 3	**32**	5 + 2	**35**	4 + 3

 Use a stopwatch or a sand timer.

Can you get
20 sums right
in 3 minutes?

Use Speedy Sums G made from Copymaster B71.

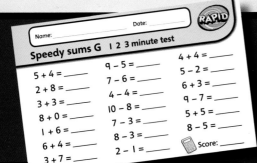

Name: _____ Date: _____ **RAPID**

Speedy sums G 1 2 3 minute test

5 + 4 = ____	9 − 5 = ____	4 + 4 = ____
2 + 8 = ____	7 − 6 = ____	5 − 2 = ____
3 + 3 = ____	4 − 4 = ____	6 + 3 = ____
8 + 0 = ____	10 − 8 = ____	9 − 7 = ____
1 + 6 = ____	7 − 3 = ____	5 + 5 = ____
6 + 4 = ____	8 − 3 = ____	8 − 5 = ____
3 + 7 = ____	2 − 1 = ____	Score: ____

Check your answers. ✔ or ✗
Count how many you got right.

Ask what to do next.

Adding up

Use tens and ones.

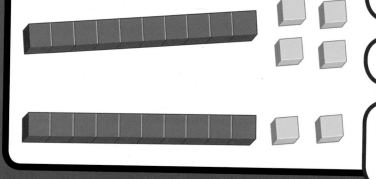

Fourteen

add twelve

is ten add ten and four add two.

$$14 + 12 = 26$$

Add up the tens and add up the ones.

Use tens and ones. Copy and complete.

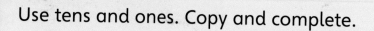

1. 12 + 17
2. 20 + 6
3. 13 + 13
4. 15 + 14
5. 11 + 15

6. 23 + 6
7. 16 + 10
8. 18 + 11
9. 10 + 15
10. 15 + 12

Addition within 40

Sometimes when you add up, you will have 10 ones, or more!

You can swap 10 ones for a ten, if you want to.

Do this with tens and ones.

15 + 17

5 add 5 makes another ten

swap!

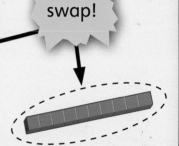

15 + 17 = 32

Use tens and ones. Copy and complete.

11	17 + 11	**13**	16 + 18	**15**	17 + 16
12	20 + 8	**14**	21 + 15	**16**	20 + 19

0, 3, 6, 9, 12, 15, 18, ...

These numbers are called <u>multiples of three</u>.

You can get <u>multiples of three</u> by adding threes, or by <u>multiplying</u> by three.

One layer of bricks

1 How many bricks?

2   ×   =

Five layers of bricks

6 How many bricks?

7 3 + 3 + 3 + 3 + 3

8 5 × 3 =

Three layers of bricks

3 How many bricks?

4 3 + 3 + 3

5   × =

Seven layers of bricks

9 How many bricks?

10 3 + 3 + 3 + 3 + 3 + 3 + 3

11 7 × 3 =

Eight layers of bricks

12 How many bricks?

13 3 + 3 + 3 + 3 + 3 + 3 + 3 + 3

14 8 × 3 =

Nine layers of bricks

15 How many bricks?

16 3 + 3 + 3 + 3 + 3 + 3 + 3 + 3 + 3

17 9 × 3 =

Thirty bricks

18 How many layers?

19 3 + 3 + 3 + 3 + 3 + 3 + 3 + 3 + 3 + 3

20 ☐ ☐ × 3 =

21 Copy and complete.

Three times table

0 × 3 =	4 × 3 =	8 × 3 =
1 × 3 =	5 × 3 =	9 × 3 =
2 × 3 =	6 × 3 =	10 × 3 =
3 × 3 =	7 × 3 =	

This is 50p ...

and this is 50p.

1. How many 10p coins make 50p?
Draw them.

2. How many 5p coins make 50p?
Draw them.

3. How many 2p coins make 50p?
Use coins to check.

How much money is in each box?

4

5

6

This is £1 ...

and this is £1.

How much money is in each box?

7

8

q

This is one pound fifty...

and so is this.

£1·50

How much money is in each box?

10

11

12

Using 50p coins and amounts over £1
Copymasters B76 and B77

Dog's toys

My dog likes toys.
They are £2 each.

1 How much for 3 toys?

2 3 × 2 =

3 How much for 5 toys?

4 5 × 2 =

5 How much for 8 toys?

6 8 × 2 =

Swimming

Holiday Special
Junior swim	50p
Adult swim	£1·00

3 juniors please.

That's £1·50 altogether.

How much will it cost?

1. 2 juniors

2. 2 adults and 2 juniors

3. 1 adult and 3 juniors

4. 4 juniors and 2 adults

5. 1 adult and 1 junior

6. 5 juniors

7. 2 adults and 3 juniors

8. 1 adult and 2 juniors

Dog food

My dog eats
2 tins of food a day.

In 3 days, she eats
<u>3 lots</u> of 2 tins.

$3 \times 2 = 6$

6 tins

1. How many tins in 4 days?

4 lots of 2 — 4 times 2 — 4 × 2

2. How many tins in 6 days?

3. How many tins in 2 days?

4. How many tins in 7 days?

5. How many tins in 5 days?

6. How many tins in 8 days?

7. How many tins in 9 days?

 ✔ or ✗

8. How many tins in 10 days?

How many days will 8 tins last?

How many 2s make 8?

Woof, woof, woof, woof!

9 How many days will 10 tins last?

How many 2s make 10? — 10 divided by 2 — 10 ÷ 2

Copy and complete.

10 ⬜ × 2 = 10

11 1 0 ÷ 2 =

12 How many days will 14 tins last?

Copy and complete.

13 ⬜ × 2 = 14

14 1 4 ÷ 2 =

Multiplication and division by 2
Copymasters B82 and B83

Taking away

Use tens and ones.

Twenty-four take away eleven is thirteen.

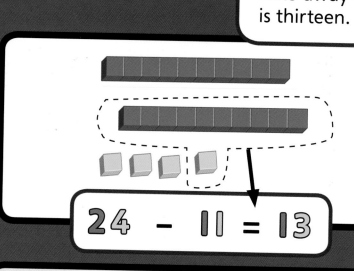

$24 - 11 = 13$

Make each number with tens and ones.

Copy and complete.

Thirty-six	**1** 36 – 14
Twenty-nine	**2** 29 – 17
Nineteen	**3** 19 – 18
Twenty-six	**4** 26 – 13
Thirty-three	**5** 33 – 13

I had 34p.
I spent 12p on an ice pop.

So you had 22p left!

34p − 12p = 22p

Use tens and ones.

How much did each person have left?

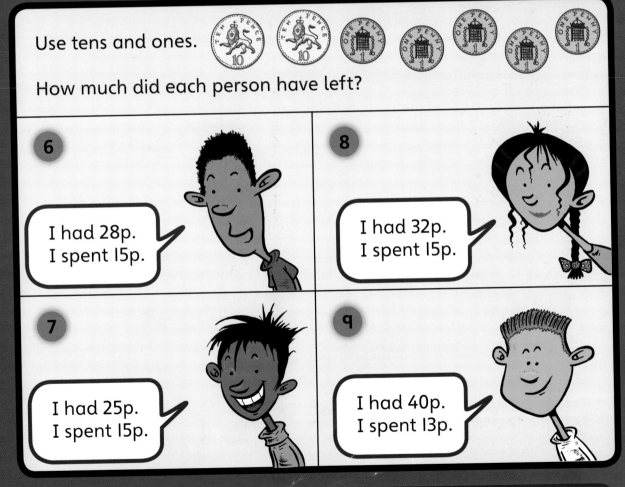

6 I had 28p.
I spent 15p.

8 I had 32p.
I spent 15p.

7 I had 25p.
I spent 15p.

q I had 40p.
I spent 13p.

Talk to your partner about how you did questions **8** and **q**.

Secret numbers

You need cards numbered 1 to 20.

I'm thinking of a number. It is smaller than 11.

It is bigger than 7.

It is an odd number.

1 2 3 4 5 6 7 8 9 10

8 9 10

It's 9

Find the secret numbers. Use cards.

1

I'm thinking of a number. It is smaller than 9. It is bigger than 5.

It is a multiple of 3.

2

I'm thinking of a number. It is smaller than 15. It is bigger than 12.

It is an even number.

3 I'm thinking of a number.
It is bigger than 10.
It is smaller than 18.

It is a multiple of 5.

4 I'm thinking of a number.
It is bigger than 6.
It is smaller than 11.

It is a multiple of 5.

5 I'm thinking of a number.
It is smaller than 17.
It is bigger than 7.

It is a multiple of 10.

6 I'm thinking of a number.
It is smaller than 19.
It is bigger than 15.

It is a multiple of 3.

Make a dozen

A <u>dozen</u> is twelve.

Find as many ways as you can to make 12.

You can add, take away, or multiply.

Write each way.
Make sure they are all different.

Make a dozen

5 + 5 + 2

20 − 8

2 × 6

7 + 1 + 1 + 1 + 1 + 1

Ask a partner to check.

✔ or ✘